WELCOME TO

DENALI

NATIONAL PARK

BY M. C. HALL

Many thanks to the staff at Denali National Park for their assistance with this book.

MAP KEY
The maps throughout this book use the following icons:

 Bear Viewing Area

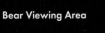 Campground

 Driving Excursion

 Hiking Trail

 Information Center

 Moose Viewing Area

 Point of Interest

 Ranger Station

 Visitor Center

 Wildflower Area

 Wooded Area

About National Parks

A national park is an area of land that has been set aside by Congress. National parks protect nature and history. In most cases, no hunting, grazing, or farming is allowed. The first national park in the United States—and in the world—was Yellowstone National Park. It is located in parts of Wyoming, Idaho, and Montana. It was founded in 1872. In 1916, the U.S. National Park Service began.

Today, the National Park Service manages more than 380 sites. Some

TABLE OF

WELCOME TO DENALI NATIONAL PARK

Λ

A LAND OF EXTREMES, 6

CHILLY HABITATS, 10

DENALI'S PAST, 14

SEASONS OF LIGHT AND DARK, 17

THE ENTRANCE AREA, 18

TRAVELING THE PARK ROAD, 21

FROM THE TOKLAT RIVER TO KANTISHNA, 24

LEAVING DENALI, 27

🚶🚶

Map, 28

Denali National Park Fast Facts, 29

Glossary, 30

To Find Out More, 31

Index, 32

A Land of Extremes

ALASKA

Denali
National
Park

Welcome to Denali National Park and Preserve! You are visiting one of the largest national parks in the United States. Denali is also one of the country's wildest and most undeveloped parks. There is only one road in the entire park—and cars aren't allowed on most of it!

You'll find that much about Denali is super-sized. Many large **mammals** live in the park, including moose, caribou, and grizzly bears. Mount McKinley, the highest mountain in the United States, is also found here.

The animals and mountains of Denali are big, but most of the plants are tiny. That's because only a few inches of soil thaw out in the summer. The rest of the ground stays frozen all year long. Many park animals depend on these plants for food. Others eat the animals that eat the plants.

 Plants such as dwarf willow and Labrador tea cover the slopes at Polychrome Pass. The Pass is a favorite stop for visitors (especially photographers) because of the area's beautiful landscape.

The morning sunlight brightens a portion of Mount McKinley's south side—an area called "Little Switzerland." In recent years, Little Switzerland has become a favorite spot with mountain climbers, who attempt to climb the difficult and dangerous rock formations.

In Denali, you will see wide, low plains and river valleys. You will also see tall, rocky mountains. The difference between the lowest and highest land is greater here than almost anywhere on Earth. In fact, if you measure from the bottom to the top of Mount McKinley, the distance is greater than at Mount Everest, the world's highest mountain! That's because the land around Mount Everest is high, and the land around Mount McKinley is low.

Earthquake Zone

Millions of years ago, earthquakes formed the Alaska Range. Every year, there are hundreds of small earthquakes near Mount McKinley. This causes the mountain to grow a tiny bit each year.

Chilly Habitats

Denali is close to the Arctic Circle, so it has a **subarctic ecosystem**. Plants and animals in the park have to be able to survive long, cold winters.

Denali's ecosystem includes several different **habitats**. Along the rivers, you'll see a **taiga** (TY-guh) habitat. There are many bushes and thick growths of spruce and willow trees. Hiking can be hard, but you can usually walk along the gravel-covered riverbeds. You may see moose, red squirrels, and even bears.

As the land gets higher, you won't see any trees. This habitat is the moist **tundra**. The ground is covered with moss and low bushes. It feels spongy when you walk across it! There are many wildflowers and berries. Caribou, fox, and bears are a few of the animals that live here.

As you climb higher in the Denali landscape, the taiga forests give way to low-growing tundra plants. All plants that live in Denali need to be able to survive the harsh winter weather and take advantage of the short summer growing season.

Dall sheep are also called "Dall's sheep" and "thinhorn sheep." Adults usually weigh about 200 pounds (91 kg) and stand 3 feet (1 m) high at the shoulder. Dall sheep have rough pads on the bottoms of their hooves that let them move easily on rough, rocky, and very steep ground.

As you go higher, you reach the dry tundra. Moss won't grow here, but there are still bushes and wildflowers. This habitat is home to animals like Dall sheep, caribou, and the arctic ground squirrel.

Denali's steep mountains are always cold and windy. You may see Dall sheep climbing the rocky slopes of this habitat. However, you won't be doing any mountain climbing. Only experts do that!

A Natural Landscape

In most areas of the United States, people bring in plants from other parts of the world. Sometimes these plants grow so well they force out native plants. This has not happened in Denali. The park plants are almost the same today as they were hundreds of years ago.

A Frozen Frog

The wood frog is Denali's only **amphibian**. In the fall, this frog buries itself in rotting leaves. During the winter, the frog freezes solid. Its heart stops beating! Special chemicals in its body keep the frog alive. When spring comes, the wood frog thaws out and hops off to find food.

Denali's Past

For hundreds of years, hunters followed **migrating** animals to the Alaska Range in the summer. The Athabascans were one group of hunters. The Athabascans named the tallest mountain "Denali," which means "high one" in their language.

In 1867, Alaska became a United States territory. Some Americans came to explore, however few made it as far north as Denali. In the late 1800s, the discovery of gold brought more people to the area. A miner named Mount McKinley after William McKinley, who was president of the United States at the time.

In 1907, Charles Sheldon came to study Dall sheep. He was excited about the many large animals he saw in Denali. Sheldon started working to make Denali a protected area. In 1917, almost 2 million acres (809,371 hectares) were set aside as Mount McKinley National Park. Only part of the mountain was in the park, however.

In 1980, another 4 million acres (1.6 million hectares) were added, including all of Mount McKinley. The park also received a new name—Denali National Park and Preserve.

William McKinley was the 25th president, serving from 1897–1901. His presidency was to last until 1904, but McKinley was shot on September 6, 1901. He died eight days later.

This photograph shows two Athabascan women with their children in 1902. Athabascans once lived only in the inner parts of Alaska, traveling in small groups as they hunted and fished for food. Today Athabascan people live in many different areas, from Alaska's coasts to Canada and the lower U.S. states.

Rock ptarmigans are common in Denali National Park. During the summer months, these birds' feathers have both light and dark colors to help them blend in with their surroundings and hide from enemies. In winter, their feathers are completely white, matching the snow and ice. Rock ptarmigans have feathered feet, which help them walk on soft snow. Only about 13 inches (33 cm) long, rock ptarmigans make their nests on the ground and eat leaves, seeds, and insects.

Seasons of Light and Dark

Summer is definitely the best time to come to Denali. Summers here are cool, however, so keep a jacket handy. Because Denali is close to the Arctic Circle, you'll have plenty of daylight. In the middle of the summer, the sun shines for almost 21 hours a day!

During the summer, birds are everywhere in Denali. Many birds come from as far away as Africa and South America. They migrate to Denali in the spring, then leave in the fall. A few birds live in the park all year, including the eagle, raven, magpie, ptarmigan, and gray jay.

By September, the weather starts getting cold. It can snow in parts of the park. Autumn quickly changes to winter, which is Denali's longest season. The temperature can fall to –40 degrees F (–40 C)!

People visit the park all year long. However, winter visitors don't see all the animals. Many animals **hibernate** or migrate to warmer places. Besides, in late December, it's dark for all but a few hours a day.

The Entrance Area

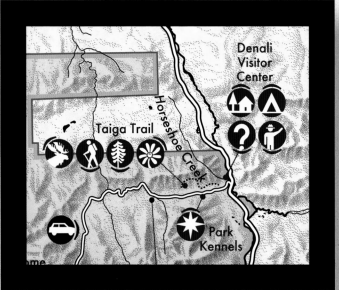

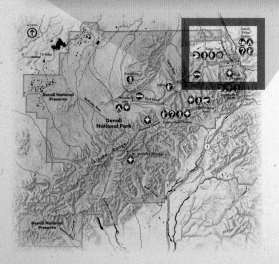

Your tour begins at the Denali Visitor Center. Check out the exhibits there. Then take a hike along the Taiga Trail. This trail goes through a forest of spruce, aspen, birch, and poplar trees. Look into the woods and you'll see a carpet of moss. If you're really lucky, you may spot a moose dipping into Horseshoe Creek for a mouthful of plants!

A short bus ride takes you from the visitor center to the park kennels. There you can visit the sled dogs and see a demonstration. The ranger hitches five dogs to a sled with wheels. Then the dogs pull the sled around a gravel track.

Most of Denali is wilderness, with no trails or roads. In the winter, the snow is deep. Rangers use sleds pulled by teams of dogs to patrol the park.

Now it's time to pitch your tent. Tomorrow you'll get on a bus to see more of Denali.

Traveling the Park Road

I t's morning—time to get on the bus. The park road is 90 miles (145 km) long, and there are lots of interesting places where you can stop and explore. You need more than one day, so bring your camping gear.

As you travel down the road, look to the left. Much of the time, Mount McKinley is hidden by clouds. If it is a clear day, the snow-covered peak is a spectacular sight!

Make a short stop at the Savage River, where the paved road ends. Take the trail downstream into the Savage River Canyon. As you walk along the riverbed, look for moose, caribou, and ptarmigan. You may even see a wolf, though they usually stay away from people.

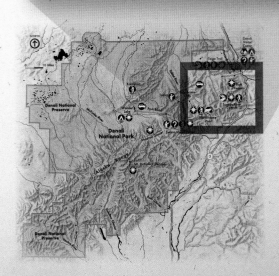

Your next stop is at Polychrome Pass. You can hike along the ridge behind the rest area. Be sure to look for caribou wandering in the river valley below. You may even spot a grizzly bear filling up on berries. Look across the valley and you'll see cliffs made up of layers of different colored rock.

Bear Safety

Here are some tips to help you stay safe in bear country.
- Make noise. Sing, whistle, or talk as you hike. If bears know you're nearby, *they* will avoid *you*!
- Be alert. If you see fresh tracks, hike somewhere else.
- If you spot a bear, give it lots of space. Stay far away!

Grizzly bears can weigh up to 1,500 pounds (680 kg) and stand over 4 feet (1 m) high at the shoulder. The bear is known for the hump on its back, which is actually a group of muscles that gives it extremely powerful front legs. Grizzlies are normally very shy animals, but they can become very dangerous when threatened. Grizzlies eat everything from berries and fish to large animals such as deer.

From the Toklat River to Kantishna

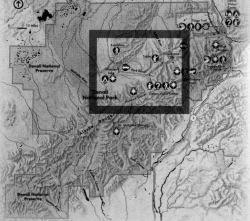

It's day two on the bus! Your first stop today is near the old Eielson Visitor Center. This is where part of Muldrow **Glacier** comes closest to the road. It's a steep hike down to the glacier, but you can do it. If you cross the stream, you can actually stand on a tip of the glacier!

The next stop is at Wonder Lake. The hills around the lake are carpeted with small shrubs and dotted with ponds. Look for gnawed tree stumps along the shores of the ponds. The marks on the trees mean that beavers have been busy. Check in the pond for a beaver lodge—a mound of sticks and mud poking out of the water. You may even see a family of beavers.

Your last stop is at Kantishna. This is the end of the road, 90 miles (145 km) from the visitor center. You can hike along the shores of the lake, which was formed by Muldrow Glacier. You will pass an old cabin that dates back to the Gold Rush, when many miners lived in Kantishna.

Thousands of people rushed to Alaska to find gold in 1898 and 1899. One place that quickly filled with gold-seekers was the Kantishna area. By the early 1900s, the rush was over, and the miners left. Today Kantishna is a quiet and beautiful place once more.

Glaciers

The steep peaks and low valleys of Denali were carved out by glaciers more than 10,000 years ago. Glaciers are large areas of slowly moving ice. They form when more snow falls in the winter than melts in the summer. The snow piles up. Layers of snow near the bottom turn to ice. Then the glacier starts to slide downhill very slowly. There are still many glaciers in the Alaska Range.

Leaving Denali

The next morning, it will be time to get on the bus to go back to the visitor center. The trip will take all day. That means you will have lots of time to look out the window at Denali's animals, plants, tundra, and mountains. Don't forget that you can come back again to explore more of this wonderful wilderness.

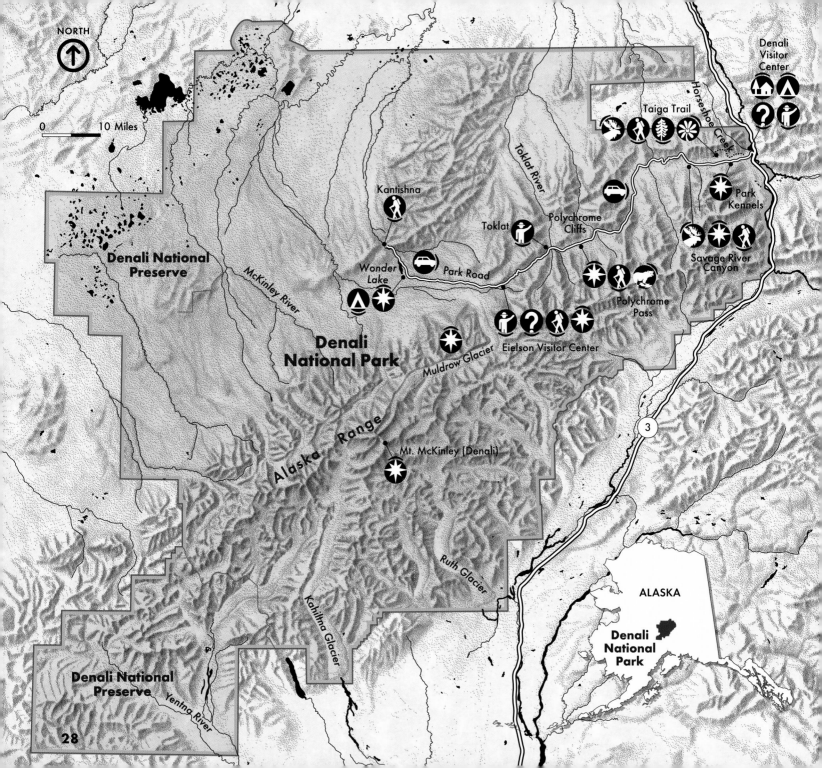

NORTH

0   10 Miles

Denali Visitor Center

Taiga Trail

Denali National Preserve

Kantishna

Toklat River

Toklat

Polychrome Cliffs

Park Kennels

McKinley River

Park Road

Wonder Lake

Savage River Canyon

Denali National Park

Muldrow Glacier

Polychrome Pass

Eielson Visitor Center

Alaska Range

Mt. McKinley (Denali)

Horseshoe Creek

3

Ruth Glacier

ALASKA

Kahiltna Glacier

Denali National Park

Denali National Preserve

Yentna River

DENALI NATIONAL PARK FAST FACTS

Date founded: February 26, 1917 (as Mount McKinley National Park; increased in size and changed to Denali National Park and Preserve on December 2, 1980)

Location: South-central Alaska

Size: More than 9,375 square miles/24,281 sq km; 6 million acres/2.4 million hectares

Major habitats: Taiga, moist tundra, dry tundra, mountain

Important landforms: Mountains, river valleys, glaciers, taiga, and tundra

Elevation:
    Highest: 20,320 feet/6,194 m above sea level (Mount McKinley)
    Lowest: 200 feet/61 m above sea level (Yentna River)

Weather:
    Average yearly rainfall: 15 inches/38 cm at the park headquarters
    Average yearly snowfall: 80 inches/203 cm at the park headquarters
    Average temperatures (at park headquarters): 66 F/19 C to –7 F/–22 C

Number of animal species: More than 200, including more than 167 kinds of birds, 1 amphibian species, 10 fish species, and 39 types of mammals; also many insects

Main animal species: Caribou, moose, dall sheep, wolves, grizzly bears, beavers, marmots, and squirrels

Number of plant species: More than 1,500, including more than 650 species of flowering plants, 8 types of trees, and about 600 different mosses, lichens, and liverworts

Main plant species: Spruce, willow, birch, aspen, moss, and alpine flowers

Number of endangered plants and animals: 0

Native people: Nomadic hunters of the Athabascan, Ahtna, Tanana, and Koyukon tribes

Number of visitors each year: More than 400,000

Important sites and landmarks: Mount McKinley, Alaska Range, Polychrome Cliffs, Muldrow Glacier, and Wonder Lake

Tourist activities: Hiking, viewing wildlife, climbing, and winter sports

GLOSSARY

amphibian (am-FIB-ee-yun): An amphibian is a cold-blooded animal that spends part of its life in or on water and part on land. Frogs, toads, and salamanders are amphibians.

ecosystem (EE-koh-sis-tum): An ecosystem is a community of plants and animals living in and adapted to a specific kind of environment, such as a desert or pine forest. Denali has a sub-arctic, or cold, ecosystem.

glacier (GLAY-shur): A large mass of slowly moving ice is called a glacier. Glaciers form in mountains where more snow falls in the winter than melts in the summer.

habitats (HAB-uh-tats): The natural surroundings of a plant or animal are its habitat. The habitats of Denali are suited for plants and animals that can survive cold winters.

hibernate (HY-ber-nayt): To hibernate is to sleep during very cold weather. Bears hibernate in caves or dens.

mammals (MAM-mullz): Warm-blooded animals that have hair or fur and nurse their young are mammals. Bears, mice, and humans are mammals.

migrating (MY-grayt-ing): Migrating animals travel from one place to another to find food, warmer weather, or to have their babies. The Athabascan people followed migrating animals to the Alaska Range.

subarctic (sub-ARK-tik): The subarctic is an area in the northern part of the world, outside the arctic circle, where it is cold. Alaska is in a subarctic region.

taiga (TY-guh): A moist, subarctic northern forest is a taiga. Spruce, willow, birch, and aspens grow in taiga forests.

tundra (TUN-druh): Tundra is flat or rolling, treeless land. Most of the tundra stays frozen all year long.

TO FIND OUT MORE

Λ

FURTHER READING

Corral, Kimbery, Hannah Corral and Roy Corral.
*My Denali: Exploring Alaska's Favorite
National Park with Hannah Corral.*
Anchorage, AK: Alaska Northwest Books, 1995.

Miller, Debbie S. and Jon Van Zyle (illustrator).
Disappearing Lake: Nature's Magic in Denali National Park.
New York: Walker and Co., 1997.

Petersen, David.
Denali National Park and Preserve.
New York: Children's Press, 1996.

ON THE WEB

Visit our home page for lots of links
about Denali National Park:

http://www.childsworld.com/links

NOTE TO PARENTS, TEACHERS, AND LIBRARIANS:
We routinely check our Web links to make sure
they're safe, active sites—so encourage your
readers to check them out!

👫 ABOUT THE AUTHOR

M.C. Hall worked for many years as a classroom teacher and reading specialist in New York State. She has also been a writer and editor for an education publisher, a consultant with the Iowa State Education Department, and executive editor of a children's toy and book company in New Hampshire. For the past ten years, Ms. Hall has been a freelance writer working for a variety of clients. She has written more than 80 nonfiction and fiction books for children, ranging from biographies to fairy tales. She has also written many teacher guides and other education materials. Presently, she lives in the Boston area.

INDEX

Alaska Range, 9, 14, 26
animals, 6, 10, 13, 14, 17, 27
Arctic Circle, 10, 17
Athabascans, 14, *15*

beavers, 24
birds, 17

caribou, 6, 10, 13, *20*, 21, 22

Dall sheep, *12*, 13, 14

earthquakes, 9
ecosystem, 10

glacier, 24, 26, *26*
gold, 14, 24, *25*
grizzly bear, 6, 22, *23*

habitats, 10, 13

Kantishna, 24, *25*

Little Switzerland, *8*

McKinley, William, 14, *14*
miners, 14, 24, *25*
mountain climbing, *8*, 13
mountains, 6, 9, 13, 27
Mt. McKinley, 6, *8*, 9, 14, *19*, 21
Muldrow Glacier, 24

park road, 6, 21
plants, 6, 7, 10, *11*, 13, 27
Polychrome Pass, 7, 22
ptarmigans, *16*, 21

Ruth Glacier, *26*

Savage River, 21
Savage River Canyon, 21
Sheldon, Charles, 14
sled dogs, 18, *19*
soil, 6
summer, 6, *11*, *16*, 17, 26

taiga, 10, *11*, 18
tundra, 10, *11*, 13, 27

winter, 10, *11*, 13, *16*, 17, 26
Wonder Lake, 24
wood frog, 13